GO EXTREME!

BE A PRO RACE CAR DRIVER

By Lynda Arnez

Gareth Stevens PUBLISHING

Please visit our website, www.garethstevens.com. For a free color catalog of all our high-quality books, call toll free 1-800-542-2595 or fax 1-877-542-2596.

Library of Congress Cataloging-in-Publication Data
Names: Arnéz, Lynda, author.
Title: Be a pro race car driver / Lynda Arnez.
Description: Buffalo, New York : Gareth Stevens Publishing, [2024] | Series: Go extreme! | Includes bibliographical references and index.
Identifiers: LCCN 2023004428 | ISBN 9781538286937 (library binding) | ISBN 9781538286920 (paperback) | ISBN 9781538286944 (ebook)
Subjects: LCSH: Automobile racing–Juvenile literature. | Automobile racing drivers–Juvenile literature.
Classification: LCC GV1029.13 .A76 2024 | DDC 796.72–dc23/eng/20230207
LC record available at https://lccn.loc.gov/2023004428

First Edition

Published in 2024 by
Gareth Stevens Publishing
2544 Clinton St
Buffalo, NY 14224

Designer: Ellen Weber
Editor: Kristen Rajczak Nelson

Photo credits: Cover, p. 1 OlegRi/Shutterstock.com; p. 5 Thor Jorgen Udvang/Shutterstock.com; p. 7 (Earnhardt Sr.) Zuma Press, Inc./Alamy; pp. 7 (Earnhardt Jr.), 9, 19, 29 Grindstone Media Group/Shutterstock.com; p. 11 Corepics VOF/Shutterstock.com; p. 13 FLUKY FLUKY/Shutterstock.com; p. 15 cristiano barni/Shutterstock.com; p. 17 Bruce Alan Bennett/Shutterstock.com; p. 21 Fabio Pagani/Shutterstock.com; p. 23 Bruce Alan Bennett/Shutterstock.com; p. 25 Jay Hirano Photography/Shutterstock.com; p. 27 Ev. Safronov/Shutterstock.com; Series Art Mind Pixell/Shutterstock.com; Series Art Duda Vasilii/Shutterstock.com; Series Art PegasuStudio/Shutterstock.com; Series Art Scott Webb/Pexels

Printed in the United States of America

CPSIA compliance information: Batch #CS24GS: For further information contact Gareth Stevens, New York, New York at 1-800-542-2595.

CONTENTS

In the Driver's Seat 4

What Does It Take? 6

Get in a Kart 12

Know the Rules 16

Put in the Work 18

Making Money 22

On the Team 26

Stay Safe 28

Get Ready to Go Pro! 30

For More Information 31

Glossary 32

Index 32

IN THE DRIVER'S SEAT

Becoming a professional race car driver is not easy. But, if zooming around a tight turn in a fast car gets you excited, you can get started now! In fact, many of the greatest drivers today started racing as kids.

PUSHING THE LIMITS

"Professional" means a person is paid to do a job.

WHAT DOES IT TAKE?

Becoming a pro race car driver takes skill. Pro drivers know how to drive on the road or track, even when it's wet. They respond quickly to changes in the car. Some people are naturally gifted as a driver, but anyone can work hard at learning it.

PUSHING THE LIMITS

Many pro drivers come from racing families. Dale Earnhardt Jr.'s father was one of the most successful NASCAR drivers ever. His grandfather raced cars too!

Dale Earnhardt Jr.

Dale Earnhardt Sr.

Driving cars at 200 miles (322 km) per hour or more is hard on the body. It can be really hot inside the car too! Plus, racing is **stressful**. Being fit and strong allows drivers to drive well in these conditions.

PUSHING THE LIMITS

Some pro race car drivers deal with **g-forces**. Paying attention during a race while withstanding g-forces takes a lot of energy, or strength and ability.

Having the will to race may not be enough to succeed at a high level. You also need money! Racing is an expensive, or costly, sport. Drivers just starting out may have to buy their own car, parts, and gear.

PUSHING THE LIMITS

Race car drivers commonly need a helmet, fireproof suit, and driving gloves.

GET IN A KART

How does a kid learn to drive? Karting is a racing sport that uses small, four-wheeled **vehicles** called karts. They are open and low to the ground. Karts are fast! Kart courses are like those pro racers take on.

PUSHING THE LIMITS

NASCAR driver Chase Elliott started racing karts when he was just 8 years old! By 15, he had won more than 60 races.

Once you're comfortable in a kart, you can start racing! Racing karts is one way to get noticed by professional racing teams. Some of them have **development** programs for young drivers. This could be the fast track to a pro racing **career**!

PUSHING THE LIMITS

Formula 1 superstar Lewis Hamilton started the McLaren Mercedes program for young drivers in 1997. He was only about 12 years old!

Lewis Hamilton

KNOW THE RULES

Now, it's time to get in a car! Drivers ages 14 to 17 need a **permit** for novices, or beginners, from the Sports Car Club of America (SCCA) or a similar group. To get the permit, you may need to take special classes or to have completed some races.

PUSHING THE LIMITS

Pros can be young! NASCAR driver Harrison Burton raced in NASCAR truck series races at 16 and 17.

Harrison Burton

PUT IN THE WORK

Once you're behind the wheel of a race car, you must practice! The more you practice, the better you'll get. That means doing lots of laps at the local track or racecourse. Some drivers practice using a driving **simulator** too.

PUSHING THE LIMITS

Some drivers go to special schools that teach how to drive a race car.

Any race—no matter how you do—helps teach the skills you need to be a pro. A driver needs to compete, or try to win, in a certain number of races to earn a competition **license**. Then, you can start entering bigger races!

PUSHING THE LIMITS

Big races can cost a lot of money to enter. You may need another job to pay for your racing costs until you go pro—and maybe for a time after that!

MAKING MONEY

In order to call yourself a pro, you need to get paid to race. Every race you attend is another chance to make connections, or network, with those in the racing world. This is one way to get endorsements!

PUSHING THE LIMITS

Endorsements are deals drivers make with companies for money or gear. The drivers then must wear a company's gear, drive its cars, or appear in ads for it.

Winning races is the best way to get endorsements. Companies want their name connected to people who are doing well and are well known. Having a big social media following can draw endorsements too, even if you aren't winning yet.

PUSHING THE LIMITS

Endorsements may cover the cost of entering the biggest races. They may pay for car parts and maintenance, or the upkeep and fixing of your car.

ON THE TEAM

Race car drivers that are part of a team may make a salary too. That means they are paid a certain amount of money every year to drive for the team. Formula 1 drivers may earn even more money from their team if they win!

PUSHING THE LIMITS

In 2022, F1 driver Charles Leclerc earned more than $20 million driving for Ferrari—and that doesn't include his endorsements.

Charles Leclerc

STAY SAFE

Top pro race car drivers make a lot of money! They also put themselves in danger. Crashes happen and can end careers, and even lives. You can get started racing now, but always follow the safety rules when you're behind the wheel!

PUSHING THE LIMITS

Pro drivers who win races get prize money too! IndyCar star Marcus Ericsson got $3.1 million for winning the 2022 Indianapolis 500.

Marcus Ericsson

GET READY TO GO PRO!

You can start your journey to becoming a pro race car driver today!

Get fit!

Running, swimming, and lifting weights can help you be more fit for race car driving.

Start kart racing!

Talk to your family about learning to drive a kart.

Join a racing club.

Find out if your community has a racing club that puts on races for kids.

Earn and save money.

Do jobs for your family and neighbors. Save the money to buy new gear and pay to enter races when you are ready.

FOR MORE INFORMATION

BOOKS

Abdo, Kenny. *Bubba Wallace*. Minneapolis, MN: Fly!, an imprint of Abdo Zoom, 2022.

Cella, Clara. *Race Car Drivers*. Minneapolis, MN: Lerner Publications, 2023.

WEBSITES

F1 – The Official Homepage of Formula 1® Racing
www.formula1.com/
Follow all the top F1 drivers here.

Sports Car Club of America
www.scca.com/pages/i-want-to-road-race
Find out what you need to do to get the right permits and licenses to race through the Sports Car Club of America.

Publisher's note to educators and parents: Our editors have carefully reviewed these websites to ensure that they are suitable for students. Many websites change frequently, however, and we cannot guarantee that a site's future contents will continue to meet our high standards of quality and educational value. Be advised that students should be closely supervised whenever they access the internet.

GLOSSARY

career: A job someone does for a long time.

development: The state of getting better over time.

g-force: The force of gravity or acceleration (speeding up) on the body.

license: A document that allows someone to do something.

permit: A document from a government or organization that allows someone to do something. In driving and racing, it may have limits on it.

simulator: A tool or device that allows the user to put themselves under the conditions and situations one might experience driving a race car.

stressful: Full of stress, or a feeling of worry.

vehicle: An object that moves people from one place to another.

INDEX

Burton, Harrison, 17
Earnhardt, Dale Jr., 7
Earnhardt, Dale Sr., 7
Elliott, Chase, 13
endorsements, 22, 23, 24, 25, 27
Ericsson, Marcus, 29
fitness, 8, 30
gear, 10, 11, 23, 30
Hamilton, Lewis, 15
karts, 12, 13, 14, 30
Leclerc, Charles, 27
social media, 24